Appreciate your Support!
~ Bennett Hendrix III

Saleen, the CyberTeen

A Cybersecurity Introduction

Bennett Hendrix III

ISBN: 978-0-578-71415-8

Table of Contents

Lesson 1:

Introduction

So, you want to learn the field we call Cyber.

Luckily, I know it so well it's in my fibers.

We will cover topics including Careers,

Networking, coding, and more will appear.

At the end of each lesson, I gave an activity.

Intended so you can get experience instantly.

These shall give you a good example.

Helping you to digest the info, like an apple.

Let me tell you the format of how this'll go.

I'll introduce these topics as best I know.

I speak in the form of simple rhymes.

This will help you learn the info in time.

You can read silently or maybe out loud.

Recite it to your parents and make them proud.

If there's hardship pronouncing a word.

Google the term so it can be heard.

Now you will be able to increase your vocabulary!

You can learn everywhere, not just the library.

If you have questions, researching the topic is advised.

I'm sure you'd learn something you'd like and be surprised.

This is a valuable skill: Researching independently.

But this information isn't supplementary.

Use me as a cyber topics' introduction.

To give you an idea of how it functions.

Getting you ahead in life, that's my goal.
Teaching cyber security is my role.
I make it rhyme so its fun to learn.
Now here I am! And it's your turn!

If my word choice cause confusion as a result,
There's a glossary at the end, you could consult.
Luckily for you, I am already on the scene.
Let's begin: Hey, I'm Saleen the CyberTeen!

Lesson 2:

Cyber Security

You can think of cyber as a big shield.
And Cyber security consists of three fields.
We will learn about each one later.

Network goes over each OSI layer.

Internet security and cyber security relate greatly.

We will discuss attacks and online safety.

In **Computer science** we will cover coding.

Cyber security will always continue growing.

Cyber security is protecting against

unwanted access.

If crimes are committed, it will lead to arrests.

There's strategy involved and it's a game of wits.

Unfortunately, you shall always prepare to be hit.

To say anything is "unhackable" is a lie.

This will attract the attention of the bad guy.

They will try to get on your network and load malware.

Fortunately, these can be prevented with some care.

A computer **program** is a collection of instructions.

Malware are programs that cause destruction.

This can be identified by a system crash.

Or maybe your computer screen will begin to flash.

Viruses can cause significant damage and more.

Please decide to take action and do not ignore.

I'll tell you what it is then how it's identified.

I'll end with some questions so you can decide.

There are many types of malware.

For starters there is **ransomware.**

Which is a virus that encrypts files for ransom.

Basically, someone locked your files and to you it's random.

Viruses can take control of your computer and add it to a **botnet.**

Which is an army of computers controlled over the internet.

There're also viruses that open **backdoors.**

Basically, secret access to the device that's yours.

The last one I'll cover is called a **logic bomb.**

It has this name because it looks to be calm.

Until it's triggered by a condition being met.

Like every time the computer is reset.

Computer **viruses** are attached to programs and hidden.

Majority are on Windows, that's just how they're written.

Worm is a type of malware that spread without interaction.

Unlike viruses, it spreads itself, and have a chain reaction.

Always be on the lookout, you can fall victim.

So, here I go: Giving you some wisdom.

Here's a couple questions to help you determine.

If so, you may have a virus on your PC that's current.

Is your computer now slow? That's an indicator.

Act fast or a mysterious shutdown may occur later.

Do you see new programs that you didn't install?

This is one of the biggest indicators of them all!

A few more signs are unwanted browser toolbars.

Random websites that are mysteriously bookmarked.

Unknown files that have been recently downloaded.

Websites you reach are not the ones you've chosen.

Have you notice any files that disappeared?

What about other behaviors that seem weird?

IP addresses are strings of numbers separated with a period.
These are the location of your network.
Best kept hid.

These help websites know where to deliver the info.
Your city, state, and country reports back to the window.
This can be used when an attacker knows their target.
They'll chose an attack method over the Internet.

A **network** is when your devices speak to each other.

Using IP and MAC addresses to reach one another.

MAC addresses are given when the device is created.

Manufacturers assigns the media access control numbers stated.

Activity
Find your IP address by Googling: What's my IP address.
You should receive a string of numbers to show success.
Or go to Start menu -> Run -> CMD -> and type ipconfig.[1]
Now you know what your IP address is.

[1]Only Windows Operating systems

Lesson 3:

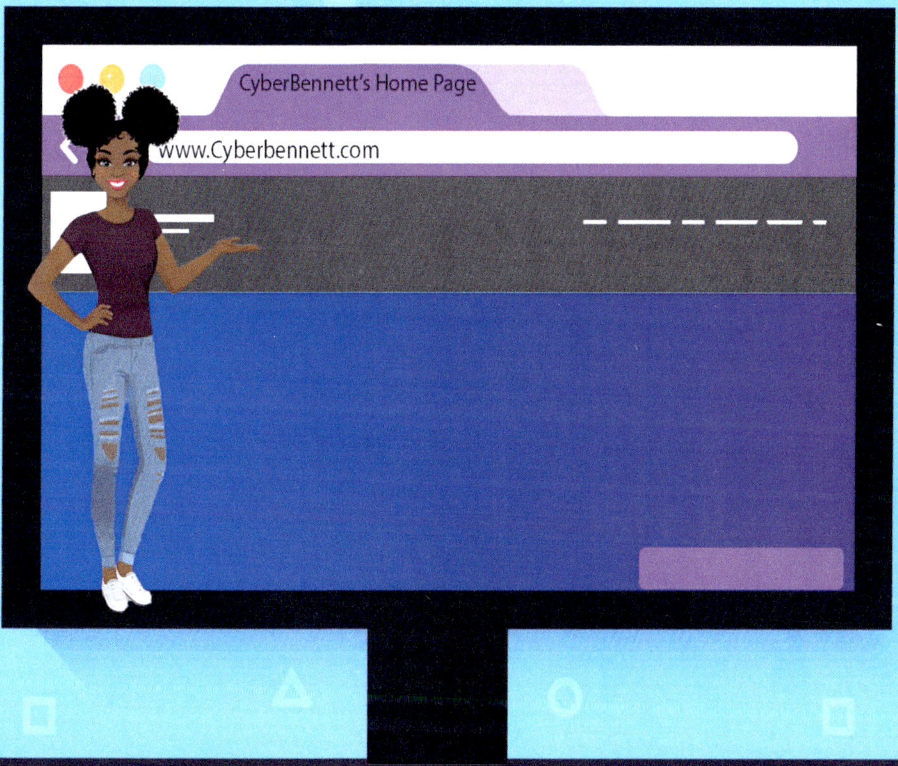

Online Safety

There are many misconceptions regarding being hacked.

People always think it is a sophisticated attack.

When in reality its usually simple tactics.

Sharing passwords and info is problematic.

A password should be pretty hard to guess.

If they are able to, you will become stressed.

That's how they get into your account and steal.

Your information. They will take anything ideal.

A difficult password is long and uses symbols.

Include your favorite number in the middle.

If you have many, use a password manager.

That will make managing passwords much simpler.

When these are used, you only need one.

One master password to remember and you're done.

You can find and get these programs for free.

It's really easy to install them on your PC.

Speaking of which, lets talk about games.

Only trust websites with the same name.

So, even if you only installed Pac-Man.

After every download, give your computer a scan.

Anti-virus is a software that will remove

Any program that it's vendor disapprove.

This is done because the programs check a list.

A list of bad programs your security tools may have missed.

Don't go to bad or unknown websites!

Make sure you type the address right.

Sometimes an error will display.

Seek the green bar, anytime you pay.

This tells you that the site is pretty secure.

Before buying anything, please make sure.

Or mommy's credit card info may be taken.

And her account will have a break in.

Nothing online is free. Just so you know.

Those false, bright banners are just for show.

If you do click them, then you'll get a **pop up.**

This is a window that keeps popping up.

I don't hope this comes as a shocker.

But this can be prevented with an ad-blocker.

Do not upload pictures. They never delete.

So, no embarrassing pictures of your feet.

Oh, and don’t confuse the meaning of the **cloud**.

Whether its OneDrive, Google Drive, or iCloud.

Basically, it’s using someone’s computer to store your files.

Trying to identify the computer may take a while.

Internet Security is something that is required.

You must know what hackers desire.

Establishing rules to defend against online attacks.

In order to do this, you will need to know the facts.

Defining web attacks is what we will do first.

Unsecure websites are the worst.

Identifiable by looking at the web address.

HTTP websites are calling out SOS.

Fortunately, secure websites are enforced indeed.

These provide encryption that these sites need.

Encryption is when your data is scrambled.

That's how HTTP should be handled.

HTTP websites send data in plaintext.

Which attackers can read and detect.

Detecting the information sent to the website.

This is how they steal credentials downright.

HTTPS is the protocol responsible for data transmission.

This hides your data even if they decide to listen.

The most commonly used security method is encryption.

Which needs the key that is required for decryption.

Do you know about the **Internet of Things**?

These are important as more are being seen.

These are hackable and used to spy.

Basically, it’s anything connected to the Wi-Fi.

For example: Alexa or Google home.
These are inoperable once you roam.
So, In other words smart devices.
Do not let these cause a crisis.

These are great gifts to give and to receive.
But just make sure that you do not leave
The default password. It's vulnerable.
This can make your network discoverable.

Default passwords can be found on websites.
Try your best to make your security air-tight.
This is a fairly common mistake.
So please change the password for goodness sake!

There is a common online attack called **phishing.**

It's pronounced the same, but not the same as fishing.

Phishing is when they get your info using trickery.

Not responding to them, ensures your victory.

However, these perpetrators are becoming

Increasingly sophisticated so they're cunning.

Verifying caller's identity is the best defense.

Ignoring their call will beat their offense.

Falling victim or recognizing them is not hard.

They will do what they can to get your debit card.

By telling you to confirm your identity.

Or checking the address for your billing.

They may ask you to download software for remote access.

You can know this if they ask for your IP address.

Usually they act as if they're apart of IT.

And give a service like removing malware for a fee.

They may also direct you to their websites.

This will allow them to get paid and win the fight.

If a message claims you have a virus on your monitor.

Find the close button in the corner and go as you were.

When you are in public, use privacy screens.

These prevent people looking over and seeing

Important information, called **shoulder surfing.**

This is common, whether or not you're working.

There are different attacks devoted to passwords.

Hopefully, some of these, you have heard.

Dictionary attack is one that uses words in a dictionary.

This is why using words as passwords is scary.

Brute force uses trial and error to achieve its objective.

It will use any method that seems to be effective.

Or the top 100 most common passwords list.

Or a dictionary attack to assist.

These attacks are why passwords need to be complex.

That's why we add numbers and symbols to our text.

They also recommend using passphrases.

Its incredibly secure and deserve the praises.

Activity

In addition to screens, you can lower your brightness.

Privacy screens are cheap, but this tactic is priceless.

The following is something you can search on your own.

Answer me this: Are these screens available for your cell phone?

Lesson 4:

Mobile Devices

Now let's talk a little about cell phones.

You can take these away from your home.

But there is more that you can do as well.

There are many apps that are on your cell.

If you have an android, go to Google Play.

For iPhone owners, App Store is the way.

Using other resources puts you at risk.

These are concerns you should not dismiss.

Both stores remove apps that violate their policies.

Why would you want to reduce your phone's quality?

In case you don't want to follow this suggestion.

I will add another tip to ensure your protection.

Only download from sites that are trustworthy.

Androids or jailbroken phones cause worry.

Jailbreaking iPhones voids the warranty.

This also ruins the established security.

When using a pin, do not choose 4 digits.

If entered wrong, it should lock for some minutes.

For difficulty, 6 or more digits is preferred.

If able, add a couple letters or a word.

Mobile phones have the benefit of **biometrics.**

This is a security technique using your genetics.

Whether its your thumbprint or facial recognition.

It removes remembering passwords upon submission.

There are apps that have fraud detection.

They add new spam callers to their collection.

Having an anti-virus app is good practice.

Make sure your security apps are active.

Virtual Private Network may be most crucial.

This is a resource that is incredibly useful.

VPN, in short, encrypts your traffic.

This is done to hide your online actions.

Most mobile devices have a setting for encryption.

This is a free benefit that is already built in.

Difficult to extract and decipher info, if stolen.

Consider this ability before your device is chosen.

If you don't have a VPN, beware of public WIFI.

This is how your activity can be seen by the bad guy.

Anyone can scan the Wi-Fi with a **network sniffer.**

This is a tool that views the traffic being delivered.

Another tip always keep your apps updated.

Even though this process is usually hated.

This will improve your phone's security.

Overall improving your phone's stability.

Activity

VPNs also allow kids to bypass parental control.

Now they found a way to create a loophole.

If you are permitted to, or want to risk it.

Download a VPN and begin to test it.

Lesson 5:

Careers

Cyber security is recently established.

Finding the right position is the challenge.

There are many different types of job positions.

Two titles can have different job descriptions.

We have **Pen Testing**, which is closest to hacking.

You must get approval from those you're attacking.

They want to ensure their networks are strong.

So, they pay you to find something that is wrong.

After the results are determined.

You will no longer be a burden.

You conclude with a detailed report.

Answer any questions if they need support.

You also have the profession: **Digital forensics.**

Using their bag of tricks on digital evidence.

Recovering deleted data and hidden files.

Investigate cases and presenting on trials.

They find evidence on all sorts of devices.

Searching for criminal activity that will suffice.

Learning pen testing skills will be a benefit.

Knowing what to look for and how to get it.

Next, there is coding or programming.

Their knowledge is pretty outstanding.

They create apps, programs, and websites.

Coding takes lots of practice and rewrites.

Official title is called **software developer.**

You will get comfortable with a **debugger.**

This is a tool that test and identifies errors

Located in your code, making it work better.

You can be at the top as the CISO[2].

They are basically Cyber security CEOs.

They explain technical problems to bosses

Who want to discuss these topics often.

CISO stands for **Chief Information Security Officer.**

---

[2] Pronounced SEE-so

The highest position for their field and they monitor.

Monitoring their department and those below.

They are responsible for the company's info.

The previous section covers the positions of the career.

I'll explain what it takes to succeed, just to be clear.

It will be a great advantage, to pay attention to detail.

Solving simple obstacles quickly, allows you to prevail.

To succeed in this field, you need to be good at problem solving.

And always willing to learn, as this field is constantly evolving.

Self-educating is the fundamental way to keep up to date.

Being motivated to do so, will ensure you'll be great.

Of course, it is important to be technically capable.

Do not beat yourself up, if you are not yet able.

Instead vow to spend 30 minutes to learn something new every day.

You are halfway through this book, so technically you can count today.

There are many different ways that will last.

Like reading an article or listening to a podcast.

Playing interactive games or an audiobook will do.

Some people prefer videos. Do what best suits you.

Keep building the momentum so you are always learning.

This is a trait possessed by those with the most earnings.

Not having communication skills in this field, is a stereotype.

So, brush up on talking and explaining to people. Be polite!

Whatever you do, please do not compare

Yourself to anyone else. It is not fair.

You never know what journey they took.

That's an important tip from this book.

Activity

Because there are many different types,

Here's programming titles you may like:

App, web, and mobile to name a few.

Find some ideal positions closest to you.

Lesson 6:

Threat Actors

Anyone can be a threat actor, there's no standard.
They behave differently, some have manners.
They can be employees, students, or even hobbyists.
You can see them daily, and it still won't be obvious.

But before I try to proceed and educate,
Stay ahead of the curve and remain up to date.
Up to date with technology and methods of the **threat actors**.
They are people who cause the disaster.

There are 5 threat actors we will cover.
I'll also explain how they relate to each other.
First up is the number one threat:
Organized crime.
These are criminals who are after data or your dime.

Nation State actors are sophisticated with resources.

Sometimes different state-sponsored groups join forces.

Intellectual property is their primary objective.

Using all methods that is deemed effective.

Capable of executing attacks of a large scale.

Tracking is difficult, making them an ideal sale.

Their goals are to steal, disrupt, or spy.

Political or economic opinions determines their why.

Hacktivists are hackers who are activists.

They are goal focused and have a checklist.

From targeting their opponents to political statements.

Their motives do not involve receiving any payments.

These threat actors will display their activism.

By committing acts of cyber vandalism.

Such as a DDOS[3], **Distributed denial of service attack**.

Which is when a service or network is flooded, and jam packed.

The next one up is called: **Inside Actors.**

They are usually internal attackers.

As they act malicious, their motivation varies.

---

[3] Pronounced dēˌdôs

Employees, students, and relatives are adversaries.

Sometimes they cause problems by mistake.

Other times its intentional and they know what's at stake.

Or they were tricked by a cybercriminal.

Which is why not clicking links is critical!

Last but not least is the **Script Kiddies.**

They can be found in any city.

During an attack they leave many traces.

Mainly because they forget to cover their bases.

Despite their name, they are not children.

They are unskilled people looking for a quick win.

They buy and use programs others made for sale.

They're the first to get caught, if their attempt fail.

Nation-state is the worst; organized crime is pretty bad.

If attacked by script kiddies, just be glad.

Hacktivist attacks cause embarrassment.

Inside actors are much more relevant.

If there's a reason you can't remember the last.

Just remember hacktivists are usually in masks.

For example: You have Anonymous.

Now you can remember all five in confidence.

Activity

This activity will be focused on your ethics.

By introducing a controversial topic. Many respect it.

But, instead of giving you the term that was chosen.

I'll give you a name to research: Edward Snowden

Lesson 7:

Coding

There's plenty of languages used to code.
Learning this skill is important down the road.
Because you can create whatever you imagine.
As long as you learn, does not matter where you begin.

The best perk about coding is the return.
You determine what you want to learn.
From analyzing data to building websites.
This can be a hobby during boring nights.

There are multiple websites, so you can build your own.
And they are affordable, so you don't need a loan.
Practice makes perfect so don't try to rush.
Having patience will always come in clutch.

There are many beginner sites to get
started.
Tynker and CodeAcademy are on the
market.
Determine which options are the best.
Then you can learn and put it to the test.

Choosing which language to use will
depend.
On what your goal is in the end.
Python is high level and general purpose.
Similar to another called C++ [4].

High level means the data is easier to read.
Proper syntax is crucial compared to speed.
These are best for those who are beginners.
Using IDE helps you develop programs
quicker.

---

[4] Pronounced See Plus Plus

IDEs stand for **Integrated Development Environment.**
It can auto-fill syntax and be used to prevent
Errors. They usually have a source code editor.
And can test the program with a debugger.

If you decide programming is not your picking.
There's also something similar called **scripting.**
This is a series of commands within a file
That's able to be executed without being compiled.

Compiler is a program that translate high level
Code into a program whose execution is successful.
Basically, it converts human language into computer language.

Which is why you can use this to your advantage.

ASCII Code: Character to Binary

0	0011 0000	O	0100 1111	m	0110 1101
1	0011 0001	P	0101 0000	n	0110 1110
2	0011 0010	Q	0101 0001	o	0110 1111
3	0011 0011	R	0101 0010	p	0111 0000
4	0011 0100	S	0101 0011	q	0111 0001
5	0011 0101	T	0101 0100	r	0111 0010
6	0011 0110	U	0101 0101	s	0111 0011
7	0011 0111	V	0101 0110	t	0111 0100
8	0011 1000	W	0101 0111	u	0111 0101
9	0011 1001	X	0101 1000	v	0111 0110
A	0100 0001	Y	0101 1001	w	0111 0111
B	0100 0010	Z	0101 1010	x	0111 1000
C	0100 0011	a	0110 0001	y	0111 1001
D	0100 0100	b	0110 0010	z	0111 1010
E	0100 0101	c	0110 0011	.	0010 1110
F	0100 0110	d	0110 0100	,	0010 0111
G	0100 0111	e	0110 0101	:	0011 1010
H	0100 1000	f	0110 0110	;	0011 1011
I	0100 1001	g	0110 0111	?	0011 1111
J	0100 1010	h	0110 1000	!	0010 0001
K	0100 1011	I	0110 1001	'	0010 1100
L	0100 1100	j	0110 1010	"	0010 0010
M	0100 1101	k	0110 1011	(	0010 1000
N	0100 1110	l	0110 1100	)	0010 1001
				space	0010 0000

activity
Use the above image as a table.
Spell your name and you'll be able
To see how computers receive information.
Using binary code so you receive affirmation.

Lesson 8:

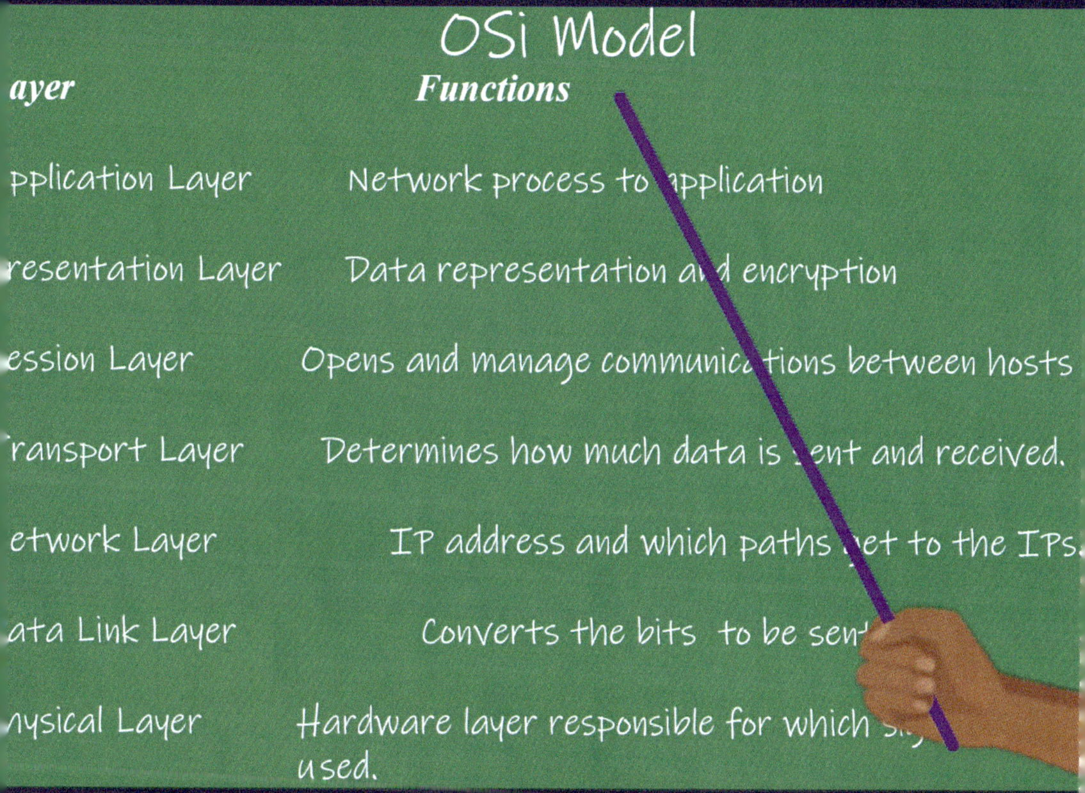

OSI Model

The OSI model is one that explains how data is transmitted.

Once the data is sent, it is committed

To finishing the process that has seven layers.

They are in a specific order, like sports' players.

We will start from bottom and finish at the top.

If one of these are skipped, the packet will drop.

The first layer we'll discuss is called: **Physical.**

This consists of objects you can touch. Typical.

Next on the list? **Data Link** is the name.

Responsible for organizing bits into **frames**.

Just another way of saying the message is cut into pieces.

Then is put together at the destination it reaches.

Third on the list is the **Network.**

This is the level that makes IPs work

It moves packets from source to destination.

Allowing you to talk to people at any location.

Fourth is a layer called **Transport.**

Decides how much info is sent. In short.

It's also reliable and sends a **checksum**.

Confirming all received errors are overcome.

And now to continue this lesson

The fifth layer is called **Session.**

It manages the communication

Between devices and their applications.

Next up, is the **Presentation** layer.

This serves as the data translator.

The last layer needs this one so that

It can read the data in the proper format.

Final layer: **Application** is what it's called.

And no, I don't mean the ones you've installed.

This is the only layer you interact with directly.

So, I want to make sure you understand correctly.

This provides many services: Like web chat,

File transfers, web surfing, and stuff like that.

It also allows access to network resources.

Does much more. Ask about it in your courses.

.*Activity*

To remember the OSI Model just say:

Please Do Not Throw Sausage Pizza Away.

Swap the words with their respective names.

And create your own phrase. Like a mini game.

So, there you have it. I hope you've
learned much.
There're many more things you may enjoy
and such.
If you'd like, allow me to visit again for
more sessions.
If you'd like, you can join cyber security as
a profession.

We've covered many things: from viruses
to jobs.
You can turn it around like doorknobs.
Remember! Don't visit unknown
websites!
Don't click on clickbait and invites!

Til Next time!!!!!

Keep growing!
and Have a

Glossary

Anti-virus: Programs that are used to protect a computer from viruses.

Backdoors: Any method by which authorized and unauthorized users are able to normal security measures and gain high privilege user access on a computer system, network, or software application.

Biometrics: Both measurement and statistical analysis a person's physical and behavioral characteristics. In biometrics authentication, personally identifiable and unique features are stored in order to give the holder access to certain resources.

Botnet: A network of computers that have been linked together by malware.

Brute force: A trial and error method wherein an application attempts to decode encrypted data, such as a password.

Checksum - A small sized number generated by checksum function used to ensure the data was not corrupted.

Chief Information Security Officer: Executive-level manager who directs strategy, operations, and the budget for the protection of the enterprise information assets and manages that program.

Cloud: A network of Internet-hosted remote servers used to store, manage, and process data in place of local servers or personal computers.

Compiler: A computer program that translates an entire set of instructions written in a higher-level symbolic language into machine language before the instructions can be executed.

Computer science: A branch of science that deals with the theory of computation or the design of computers.

Cyber Security/Cybersecurity: Measures taken to protect a computer or computer system against unauthorized access or attack.

Dictionary attack: An act of penetrating password-protected computer systems or servers using large lists of words located in a dictionary.

Digital forensics: Deals with the recovery and investigation of material found in digital devices.

Encryption: The act or process of encrypting something: a conversion of something (such as data) into a code or cipher.

Frame: A single unit of information transferred at the data link layer.

High level: A computer programming language, which is similar to a natural language (such as English) and in which each statement is translated by a compiler usually into several machine language instructions.

HTTP: A communications protocol governing the exchange of data (such as

HTML files) especially on the World Wide Web.

HTTPS: A protocol where encrypted HTTP data is transferred over a secure connection.

Integrated Development Environment: An application that facilitates application development. Designed to aid developers that are building software applications with an integrated environment that has all required tools.

Internet of Things: System of interrelated computing devices with the ability to connect and transfer data over a network.

Internet Security: Field consisting of browser security, the security of data entered through a Web form, and overall authentication and protection of data sent via Internet Protocol.

IP Address: The numeric address of a computer on the Internet.

Logic bomb: A computer program often hidden within another seemingly harmless program that is designed to perform usually malicious actions when certain conditions have been met.

Malware: Software designed to interfere with a computer's normal functioning.

Network: A system of computers and peripherals that are able to communicate with each other.

Network sniffer: Program or instrument that intercepts and logs data flowing in a network.

Packet (Network Packet) - Unit of data consisting of control information and user data.

Pen Testing/ Penetration Testing: The practice of performing controlled attacks on a computer system, network, software, or other application in an attempt to find unpatched vulnerabilities.

Phishing: A scam by which a user is fooled (usually by a deceptive e-mail message) into revealing personal information which the scammer may use illicitly.

Program: To work out a sequence of operations to be performed by a machine.

Programming: The process of preparing an instructional program for a device.

Ransomware: Malware that requires the victim to pay a ransom to access encrypted files.

Scripting: Computing a sequence of instructions or commands for a computer to execute.

Software developer: A person or company that develops computer software.

Virtual Private Network: A private network that functions over a public network and utilizes data encryption to provide secure access to something.

Viruses: A program that is usually disguised as a harmless program or file, that often produces copies of itself and inserts them into other programs, and that when run usually performs a malicious action.

Worm: A small self-contained and self-replicating computer program that invades computers on a network and usually performs a destructive action.